Joe Biden: A Short Biography

47th Vice President of the United States

By Doug West, Ph.D.

Joe Biden: A Short Biography
47th Vice President of the United States

Table of Contents

Preface

Welcome to the book, *Joe Biden: A Short Biography*. This book is part of the 30 Minute Book Series and, as the name of the series implies, if you are an average reader this book will take around 30 minutes to read. Since this short book is not meant to be an all-encompassing biography of Joe Biden, you may want to know more about this man and his accomplishments. To help you with this, there are several good references at the end of this book. Thank you for purchasing this book, and I hope you enjoy your time reading about this former Vice President of the United States.

Doug West
January 2018

Introduction

When you see a picture of a famous person or hear their name, a mental image enters your mind. For example, when you see a picture of one of the world's greatest scientists, Albert Einstein, you think of "brilliant," or when you see a picture of the German dictator Adolf Hitler, the word "evil" may pop into your mind. When you see a picture of the former vice president of the United States, Joe Biden, maybe the word "resilient" should enter your thoughts. The dictionary tells us the world resilient means, "A person able to withstand or recover quickly from difficult conditions." For Joe Biden, the word resilient fits him well.

As a young boy growing up in Pennsylvania, Joe Biden, or "Joey" as his young friends called him, had a problem with his speech. He stuttered. The problem was obvious enough that his classmates made fun of him and he had to get help from the nuns at his Catholic school to overcome the problem. Young Joey Biden would overcome this problem and become one of the most loquacious orators of his generation.

Joe Biden was a man on the move and by 1971 he had a law degree in hand, a wonderful wife, three children, and to top it off, at age 29 had won a seat in the United States Senate from his home state of Delaware. Then, in a single instance, his world changed as his wife and children were in a fatal car accident while Christmas shopping; only the two young boys would survive. The tragedy nearly forced him to give up his Senate seat. With the help of his family, he was able to stay in the Senate, making the long daily commute from Willington, Delaware, to Washington, D.C., for a career that would last for over three decades.

By 1987 Biden was ready for new challenges and threw his hat into the ring of the 1988 presidential election. His campaign didn't go well, as he was accused by his opponents of plagiarism in a speech. His hopes of becoming the youngest president since John Kennedy were dashed and he was forced from the race. His presidential aspirations would not resurface until twenty years later. In the 2008 election, he would not become president, but the vice president under Barack Obama.

Read on and see the ebbs and flows of this resilient man's life as he ascends to the second highest office in the land.

Chapter 1 - Early Life

"My dad always said, 'Champ, the measure of a man is not how often he is knocked down, but how quickly he gets up.' " - Joe Biden

Just a year after America's entry into World War II, Joseph Robinette Biden, Jr., was born into a Catholic family on November 20, 1942, in blue-collar Scranton, Pennsylvania. He was the first child of Joseph Robinette Biden, Sr., and Catherine Eugenia Biden. Joe was followed by a sister, Valerie, and two other brothers, James and Frank. His mother had Irish ancestry and his father's family descended from an English immigrant with Irish roots from Sussex, who had come to the United States a few generations before.

Joe Senior and a cousin prospered during the war working for an uncle who manufactured a watertight sealant for merchant marine ships. Business was good, so much so that both men owned the fastest new cars and piloted a small plane on hunting trips. After the war, the good times for the Biden family came to an end as Joe Senior became involved in a couple of bad business ventures with his cousin. Joe Senior's family moved into the small home of Catherine's family in the Green Ridge neighborhood made up of Irish, Italian, and Polish families. In Green Ridge, young Joe Biden or "Joey," as he was called, enjoyed a childhood of playing baseball, cops and robbers, and normal boyhood pranks while he attended a Catholic school. At the school, he was a good student but suffered from a case of stuttering, which led to ridicule from the other students. With the help of the nuns he was able to overcome the problem and later became known for his skills as an orator.

During the 1950s, Scranton and all the surrounding area went into a severe economic crisis and jobs were scarce. To find steady employment, in 1953, the Biden family moved to their own small apartment in Claymont, Delaware. Once they became secure, they bought a house in Wilmington, Delaware, and settled there. Biden, Sr., found moderate success as a car salesman and the family started to lead a comfortable, middle-class life.

Joe Biden attended Archmere Academy, a Catholic prep school in Claymont, and it was during this time that he found his talent for sports. He played football and baseball for the high school teams. From an academic standpoint, he was certainly above average. He was elected class president and was widely recognized as a natural leader. After graduating from high school in 1961, he went to the University of Delaware. Four years later in 1965, Biden earned his BA with a double major in history and political science. However, he was a mediocre college student and didn't have an outstanding academic performance.

During his junior year of college, he met Neilia Hunter while on a spring break trip to Nassau. She came from an affluent family from Skaneateles, New York, and was a student at Syracuse University. Despite the 320-mile round trip to see each other, they began dating. In order to visit her more often out of state, Biden gave up his plan of playing for the varsity football team. After getting his BA, Biden entered Syracuse University College of Law, which happened to be near Neilia's family home. He received a small scholarship due to his financial situation and managed to get additional assistance for his academic merits.

An incident occurred in his first year of law school that would come back to haunt him many years later. In his memoir, he explained, "I botched a paper in a technical writing course so badly that one of my classmates accused me of lifting passages from a *Fordham Law Review* article." Biden was called before a faculty review board to explain, and they concluded that he hadn't intentionally cheated but did require that he repeat the course. As he later revealed, he did not find law school enjoyable in the slightest and struggled to get by, calling it, "the biggest bore in the world." Into his second year of law school, Joe and Neilia were married in a Catholic Church in Skaneateles, New York, on August 27, 1966. In time, the couple would have three children, Joseph R. Biden, III, Robert Hunter, and Naomi Christina. With some help and encouragement from his new wife, he graduated in 1968 and was awarded the title of Juris Doctor. One year later, he started his own law practice, after gaining admission to the Delaware bar.

Chapter 2 - Early Political Career

"Failure at some point in your life is inevitable, but giving up is unforgivable." - Joe Biden

In 1968, Biden began working as a clerk at the law firm of the prominent Republican, William Prickett. Although he saw himself as a Republican, Biden disliked Republican presidential candidate Richard Nixon and ignored the attempts of the local Republicans to recruit him. Instead, he registered as an Independent. After being admitted to the bar, he started to practice law at another firm, led by an active Democrat, Sid Balick. Biden became a member of the Democratic Forum and changed his political party affiliation to Democrat.

Professionally, Biden was dissatisfied with his law career, even though he founded his own firm, Biden & Walsh. He did not enjoy corporate law and sought ways to supplement his income and find more interesting ventures. Near the end of 1969, Biden won a seat on the New Castle County Council, with an impressive two-thousand vote margin in the election. This was the first step of his political career, yet he already had plans for the U.S. Senate. For the next two years, he fulfilled his duties for the County Council and continued to practice law.

In 1972, Biden entered the U.S. Senate election in Delaware. Since Republican incumbent Senator J. Caleb Boggs was supported by Richard M. Nixon and by the party as well, no one among the Democrats wanted to run against him. Although he had no money for the campaign and everyone doubted that he had a chance, Biden decided to enter the race. His sister Valerie and other members of the family offered their help for the campaign. Focusing on pressing issues of the time, such as withdrawal from the Vietnam War, civil rights, protection of the environment, healthcare, foreign policies, and others, Biden gained the attention of the voters. Another plus was his young age and relentless energy when compared to Boggs, who was ready to retire. On November 7, 1972, Biden won the election. At age 29, he was not old enough by a couple of weeks to be United States Senator. However, he would reach the required age of 30 by the time of his swearing-in ceremony.

While his professional life was on an ascendant path, Biden's personal life would meet with tragedy. Just a few weeks after the election, his wife Neilia was shopping for Christmas with their three children, when a truck-trailer hit the station wagon she was driving. Neilia and their one-year-old daughter were killed while their older sons Beau and Hunter were taken to the hospital in fair condition. Devastated, Biden wanted to resign his political duties to care for his sons but was persuaded to continue by leaders in the Democratic Party. On January 5, 1973, Biden was sworn into office as a senator at the Delaware Division of the Wilmington Medical Center where his son, Beau, was still recovering from the car accident in the hospital. Biden was anxious about the demands of his new job and the drain it would cause on his already distressed family and declared he would resign "if, after six months or so, there's a conflict between being a good father and being a good senator." He told the people of Delaware, "We can always get another senator, but they [his sons] can't get another father."

Joe Biden was only 30 years old and become the sixth youngest senator in U.S. history. However, in the aftermath of the accident that killed his beloved wife and daughter, he had trouble focusing on his duties. He was doubting his religious beliefs and was crushed by great anger and grief. He left orders to be interrupted in the Senate whenever his sons called and put them above any political ambition. He commuted daily by Amtrak between his home in Wilmington, Delaware, and downtown Washington, D.C.

Figure – Official portrait of the Second Lady of the United States, Jill Biden, in 2009

Raising his two sons by himself and busy building his career in the Senate, Biden missed having a female companion in his life. While back at his home in North Star, a suburb of Wilmington, Delaware, he went on a blind date arranged by his brother with a twenty-four-year-old woman named Jill Tracy Jacobs. Their first date was for dinner and a movie in Philadelphia. As Biden would later recount the evening, "Jill showed no interest in politics. She didn't ask a single thing about my career, about Washington, about the famous people I'd met." For the next two years they dated and were married in 1977. The couple had one daughter, Ashley Blazer. Biden talked repeatedly with gratitude about how Jill reawakened his interest in politics and life in this dark period of his life. Jill would continue her education and receive multiple college degrees, including a doctorate in education from the University of Delaware, and she worked as a community college teacher in Delaware. Jill continued teaching and was embraced by the two boys as their second mother. Biden and Jill are Roman Catholics and attend church regularly.

Chapter 3 - Career in the U.S. Senate

"Given a fair shot, given a fair chance, Americans have never, ever, ever, ever let their country down. Never. Never. Ordinary people like us. Who do extraordinary things." - Joe Biden

When the young Senator Biden from Delaware took office in January of 1973, America was in a mess. The Vietnam War, which had been dragging on for years, was finally coming to a close and thousands of young men and women weary of war would come streaming back to their homes looking to find their place in society. Richard Nixon was president and 1973 would see the Watergate scandal make headlines in every newspaper in the land and the scandal endlessly debated on every television news program. The same month, as Biden entered office, the Supreme Court issued a landmark decision that would invalidate the states' abortion laws in the case of *Roe v. Wade*. This decision would cause Biden considerable consternation as this decision went against his Catholic faith. The fall of 1973 would mark the beginning of the "energy crisis" as the Organization of Arab Petroleum Exporting Countries (OAPEC) placed an oil embargo on the United States and other countries sympathetic to Israel. Americans would see shortages of gas, long lines at the gas pumps, and sky-high energy prices over the next few years.

Once in place in the Senate, Biden was primarily interested in consumer-protection legislation and he also focused on environmental issues. Fellow politicians and media characterized him as confident and ambitious. As a freshman senator in mid-1974, Biden was named one of the "200 Faces of the Future" by *Time* magazine. One of his first important legislative accomplishments was helping the passage of the Comprehensive Crime Control Act. He changed several of the Act's provisions, for which he was later praised. Biden clashed with the Reagan administration especially on foreign policies, yet he always stood his ground and was appreciated for having coherent political goals and views.

While on a speaking tour in February 1988, Biden began to suffer from severe neck pain. The pain had been manageable up until this point and Biden had already seen a doctor thinking it was from a pinched nerve. He wrote later of the incident that he remembered having felt a "sharp stick in the back of my neck and something like lightning flashing inside my head, a powerful electric surge—and then a rip of pain like I'd never felt before. I could still feel the waves of dull ache from that first blast of pain." He was taken to the Walter Reed Army Medical Center and diagnosed with an intercranial aneurysm at the base of his brain. The condition was life-treating and he underwent emergency surgery to repair the leakage within his brain. The situation was serious enough that a Catholic priest was called to his bedside to administer last rites. A second aneurysm and subsequent surgery would keep him out of the Senate for seven months. After his recovery, he plunged headlong into his work, winning approval of a major anti-drug bill and creation of a national drug czar.

***

Biden was a long-time member of the U.S. Senate Committee on the Judiciary, serving as chairman of the committee or as ranking minority member from 1981. He became deeply involved in two contentious U.S. Supreme

Court confirmation hearings. The first occurred in 1987 with the nomination of Robert Bork.

Shortly after Supreme Court Justice Lewis Powell announced his retirement, President Ronald Reagan nominated Robert Bork to fill the open position. Bork was a conservative and the Democrats took the position he was an extremist. Senators Ted Kennedy and Biden led the charge in the Senate against Bork, along with a well-funded media campaign to convince the public that Bork was too far to the political right for the position on the Supreme Court. In October of 1987, the senate voted against Bork and denied him the seat on the nation's highest court. Bork was unhappy with his treatment in the nomination process and resigned his appellate-court judgeship the next year.

In the summer of 1991, Biden found himself in the middle of another quarrelsome political fight to fill the vacancy of the retiring Justice Thurgood Marshall, the first African-American Supreme Court Justice. To fill the vacancy, President George H.W. Bush nominated another African-American, the ultra-conservative federal judge Clarence Thomas. The Democrats viewed Thomas as the most radically conservative jurist in the country and set in for a fight. Biden and his party members feared that if Thomas won a position on the highest court in the land, he would radically change the ideological composition of the court.

Figure – Justice Clarence Thomas in 2004

The course of the nomination hearings became more heated when a former subordinate of Thomas, Anita Hill, came forward with sexual harassment allegations. Thomas claimed that the charge had "done a grave and irreparable injustice" to him and his family. Despite Hill's testimony and the testimony of other black women who said they had heard of other sexual escapades of Thomas, he was narrowly confirmed by the Senate as a Supreme Court Justice.

The Thomas nomination did bring one of America's "dirty little secrets" to the forefront of the public, which was sexual harassment in the workplace. During the Thomas hearings, Anita Hill's credibility was severely attacked. In a 2017 interview, Biden would look back on that time and remark, "And my one regret is that I wasn't able to tone down the attacks on her by some of my Republican friends...I mean, they really went after her. As much as I tried to intervene, I did not have the power to gavel them out of order."

***

From the very beginning of his long career in the Senate, Biden sought a seat on the Foreign Relations Committee. It would take two more years and require the assistance of Senate Majority Leader Mike Mansfield before Biden would get his seat on the committee. He was subsequently placed on the Senate Intelligence Committee and the Judiciary Committee.

In the early 1990s, the southeastern European country of Yugoslavia was staring to unravel, and it appeared as though the country's ethnic and religious factions were bound for a bloody confrontation. Yugoslavia had been patched together by the major powers after World War I. The country was a tapestry of religion-based cultures, with Roman Catholicism, Eastern Orthodoxy, and Islam forming three distinct ways of life for the people. With the death of Yugoslavia's long-time president Marshal Tito, the country fell under the leadership of Serbian Communist leader Slobodan Milošević. The country quickly began to tear apart at the seams with Slovenia first declaring its independence, then Bosnia, and Herzegovina in a March 1992 referendum. In response to the extremely volatile conditions in the country, the

United Nations issued an arms embargo in the hopes of preventing bloodshed.

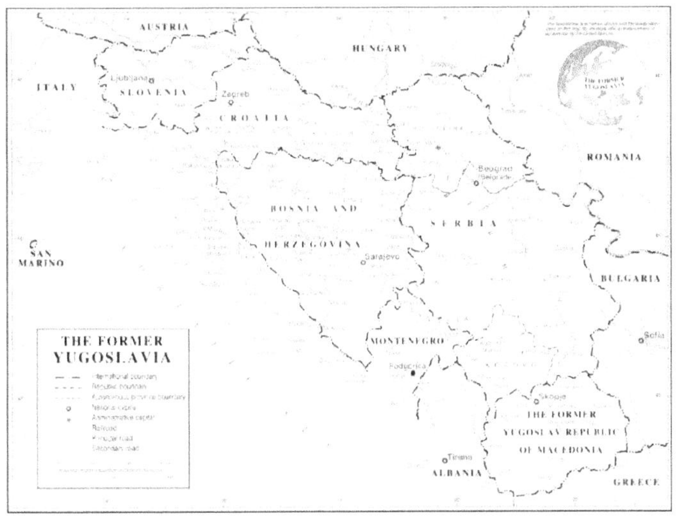

Figure – Map of the former Yugoslavia

Milosevic and his henchmen began an ethnic cleansing campaign against Croats and Muslims in Bosnia. The United Nations arms embargo left the Serbs, the majority faction in the Yugoslav army, with a strong hand. When news of the atrocities of massive concentration and death camps reached Biden, he pressed the George H.W. Bush administration to take action. Biden pushed for a lifting of the arms embargo to give the Bosnians the means of defending themselves and called for air strikes on Serb positions encircling Bosnian cities.

Biden was given the opportunity to witness firsthand what was going on in Yugoslavia when he received an invitation for a face-to-face meeting with Milošević. With approval of the Foreign Relations Committee, Biden, three staff aides, and a military attaché flew to Yugoslavia in April 1993 for a view of the situation on the ground and the meeting with the despot leader. In visiting schools and a refugee camp in Bosnia, Biden learned firsthand of the brutal atrocities against the Bosnian population.

The meeting with Milošević took place in his office in the presidential palace. The subsequent discussion didn't go all that well as Biden knew that Milošević was clearly lying about the situation. Biden would later write of the meeting, "Milošević could tell I had just about had it with his lies, and at one point he looked up from the maps and said, without emotion, 'What do you think of me?' " Biden replied: "I think you're a damn war criminal and you should be tried as one."

Upon returning to the United States, Biden, along with his fellow senator, William Roth, called for NATO to bomb the Serbian artillery positions surrounding the city of Sarajevo and for the United Nations to lift the arms embargo. It would be three years before the Senate would take action and NATO planes would begin bombing Serb positions in Bosnia. The bombing forced Milošević's hand and he agreed to peace terms in November 1995.

Milošević, still in power, would now turn his attention to the ethnic cleansing of the neighboring state of Kosovo. In March 1999, Biden introduced a resolution in the Senate authorizing President Clinton to take military action against the ethnic cleaning of Kosovo. The military action forced Milošević to withdraw his army and accept NATO troops into the province to control the region. Justice was finally served as Milošević was indicted in May 1999 by the UN's International Criminal Tribunal for the Former Yugoslavia for crimes against humanity in Kosovo and he would die in prison.

***

Into his fifth six-year term in the Senate, on September 11, 2001, America came under attack from terrorists. Using hijacked jet aircraft full of passengers, terrorists crashed the planes into the twin towers of the World Trade Center in New York City and the Pentagon in Washington, D.C., and a fourth hijacked commercial jet crashed in the Pennsylvania countryside, resulting in thousands of deaths. Just a few hours after the attacks, President Bush issued a statement, “The resolve of our great nation is being tested," he said, “but make no mistake. We will show the world that we will pass this test.” Biden supported President George W. Bush’s determination to bring to justice the perpetrators of the horrific attack.

In an attempt to prevent another attack on America, the Bush Administration focused its attention on removal of Iraq’s strongman leader Saddam Hussein. Based on flawed intelligence reports, the U.S. and its allies readied for an invasion of Iraq to remove Hussein from power and destroy his alleged massive stockpile of weapons of mass destruction. In the Senate, Biden held committee meetings to explore the implications of Bush’s strategy. Biden question, “When Saddam Hussein is gone, what would be our responsibilities [thereafter]?” He also wondered “whether resources can be shifted to a major military enterprise in Iraq without compromising the war on terror in other parts of the world.”

A political battle raged within Congress between those who wanted force used in Iraq and the camp that wanted to limit Hussein through diplomacy and sanctions. Biden wanted to give Bush the authority to disarm Saddam Hussein only if other means failed. In October of 2002, Biden voted for a resolution that gave Bush the authority for use-of-force in Iraq. Biden later said of his vote, "I thought it would give him a stronger hand to get Saddam Hussein to act responsibly, and it was a very bad bet I made."

Figure - U.S. Army M1A1 Abrams tanks and their crews pose for a photo in front of the "Victory Arch" monument at Baghdad's Ceremony Square in November 2003

In late March of 2003, the U.S. and coalition forces began what was known as the "Operation Shock and Awe" assault on Iraq. The forces quickly dispersed Iraqi forces and drove Hussein into hiding. It would be the end of 2003 before Hussein would be captured. Now the long, deadly, and expensive process of rebuilding Iraq would begin, and the process would last for years.

***

During his six terms in the Senate, Joe Biden became the longest-serving senator in Delaware history, yet he was repeatedly ranked as one of the least wealthy senators. During his time as a public official, he became known as a loquacious and confident politician, with strong public speaking skills, but who had weak filters and often said inappropriate things.

Chapter 4 - Reaching for the White House

"No one ever doubts that I mean what I say. The problem is I sometimes say all that I mean." - Joe Biden

Like all those who seek to enhance their place in the world, Joe Biden was no different. As a senator, the next rung up the political ladder was the office of the president and in mid-1987, Biden felt it was time for him to run for the Democratic presidential nomination in the 1988 election. His undeclared goal was to enter history as the youngest president since John F. Kennedy. At the start of the campaign, his goal seemed possible to attain and he was considered a strong candidate. He had a high-profile position as chair of the Senate Judiciary Committee and managed to obtain an impressive $1.7 million through fundraising. Despite an initial successful phase, his campaign suffered a big hit in September 1987, when he was accused of having plagiarized the speech of a British politician. Several other accusations of plagiarism emerged shortly and a plagiarism incident from his years in law school was brought to the public attention. Since he hadn't yet gained the support of a strong demographic group or political group, Biden's campaign went through a crisis that forced him to quit the race, and on September 23, 1987, he officially withdrew. Biden commented on the election, "There will be other presidential campaigns but there may not be other opportunities for me to influence President Reagan's choice for Supreme Court." It would be nearly twenty years before Biden would seriously entertain presidential aspirations again.

On January 31, 2007, Joe Biden officially declared his candidacy for President of the United States. During the campaign, he stressed his expertise in foreign policy to stand out as a candidate. The campaign developed successfully in the beginning, but some of Biden's remarks stirred controversy. Biden stressed his foreign policy experience compared to Obama's, saying, "I think he can be ready, but right now I don't believe he is. The presidency is not something that lends itself to on-the-job training." He struggled with raising funds and attracting people to his rallies, which kept him below double digits in the national polls in the Democratic nomination race. In the first primary vote in Iowa, Biden finished fifth, gathering less than one percent of the vote, and dropped out of the race. That evening, he said of the loss, "There is nothing sad about tonight...I feel no regret." Although defeated, Biden's position on the political scene changed for the better after his withdrawal since he now had the attention of the voters and the media. The most surprising change occurred in his relationship with Barack Obama. The two senators had worked together before, but only during the 2007 campaign managed to get close and learned to appreciate each other.

In late January, Obama approached Biden to help with his campaign. Biden declined Obama's offer, stating that he intended to remain neutral until the party nomination was complete. "If you win," he told Obama, "I'll do anything you ask me to do." According to Biden, Obama said, "Be careful, because I may ask you a lot...The only question I have is not whether I want you in this administration, it's which job you'd like best."

Biden was not initially interested in the position of vice president and declined Obama's first request to be vetted for the position. He soon changed his mind and in a June 22, 2008, interview on NBC's *Meet the Press*, Biden confirmed that he had not actively pursued a spot on the Obama ticket; however, he would accept the vice president nomination if offered.

Figure – Joe Biden and Barack Obama during the 2008 presidential campaign

In August 2008, Barack Obama publicly announced that fellow Democrat Joe Biden would be his running mate for the White House. By accepting Obama's offer, Biden also had to accept that he could not run for the presidential nomination in 2012. When candidate Obama chose Biden as his running mate, the field was down to four finalists: Senator Evan Bayh of Indiana, Governor Tim Kaine of Virginia, Governor Kathleen Sebelius of Kansas, and Senator Joe Biden of Delaware. Biden was a good choice since he countered Obama's weaknesses. For Obama's lack of experience in Washington, only three years in the Senate, Biden was a veteran Washington insider with 36 years in the Senate as well as significant experience in foreign-policy making. The two shared several positions in common; like Obama, Biden was pro-choice which ran counter to his Roman Catholic faith, and both were deeply concerned about civil rights and global AIDS prevention. On August 27, at the Democratic National Convention, Biden was officially nominated as the Democratic Party candidate for the vice presidency. This time, the campaign ran more smoothly as Biden tried to be succinct in his speeches. He avoided making offhand remarks although, on occasion, Obama grew frustrated with him, condemning his public comments.

Challenging the Obama-Biden ticket were Republicans John McCain and Sarah Palin. McCain, running for the slot as president, was a senator from Arizona with decades of political experience. Biden knew McCain well and described him as “genuinely a friend” and a courageous war hero. The Republicans introduced a charismatic and aggressive newcomer to the national political slate, Governor Sarah Palin of Alaska. The media became enthralled with Palin as she was a fresh face in the political campaign. Biden’s visibility suffered in the race, receiving far less media attention than the three other candidates. Biden focused his campaign on the economically challenged areas of swing states, trying to win over the blue-collar Democrats who had supported Hillary Clinton.

On November 4, 2008, Barack Obama was elected President of the United States and Biden was also re-elected to the Senate on the same night, since Delaware law permitted him to take the position even as vice president. However, on January 15, he resigned from the Senate. The Obama-Biden ticket had won the race with a respectable 53 percent of the popular vote and more than the required votes in the Electoral College.

During the transition period, after the election and before inauguration in the following January, he went about the task of setting up his administrative staff. Biden's plan was to "restore the balance" in the vice presidency, wanting to return it to its normal subordinate role, as opposed to his predecessor, Dick Cheney, who was allowed to take a more active role in the Bush administration. Biden began staffing the vice president's office with specialists in foreign and diplomatic policy and economic affairs that paralleled the president's staff. Biden's approach was to integrate his staff into that of the White House rather than to create a separate power structure that had evolved under Dick Cheney.

Chapter 5 - Vice President of the United States

"Here at home, when Americans were standing in long lines to give blood after the attack on the World Trade Center and the Pentagon, we squandered an obvious opportunity to make service a noble cause again and rekindle an American spirit of community." - Joe Biden

On January 20, 2009, Biden was sworn in as the 47th Vice President of the United States, alongside President Barack Obama. He accomplished his goal of making history, but not as the youngest president of the U.S. but as the first Roman Catholic and the first politician from Delaware to become vice president.

Figure – Official portrait of Vice President Joe Biden

Not long after his inauguration, Biden appeared on *Larry King Live* where he described his role as vice president and told King what he said to Obama when he was offered the vice presidency, "I want to be there when you make every critical decision you make. I want to be in the room. Because I have a significant amount of experience. I'd like to be able to give my input. You're president; if you conclude my judgment is not the right judgement, I'll abide by that, but I want an opportunity to have input."

When the Obama administration took office in 2009, the country's economy had deep problems. The significant downturn had started late in the second term of President George W. Bush and had progressively worsened going into the start of Obama's term. The main driver of the severe recession was the housing market collapse; housing prices had peaked on cheap money from the banks, and when the prices of houses fell, it was dramatic. As a result, Americans were losing their homes, their health care, and their life savings. To make things worse, local, state, and federal tax revenues were down, putting further budget pressure on the new administration. The wars in Iraq and Afghanistan were also still ongoing.

Obama tasked Biden with being the key member of the government economic team assigned to revive the aligning economy. The situation was so dire that the economic team met in the Oval Office for an hour each day to stem the tide of the unfolding crisis. The government's response, known as the American Recovery and Reinvestment Act, was a series of financial programs to inject money into the economy to simulate jobs to stop the downturn. Vice President Biden became the prime contact for state and local officials around the country in tracking the problems as they unfolded.

Shortly after taking office, Obama sent Biden to the annual European conference of security in Munich, Germany. There, Biden reported on the new president's determination "to set a new tone not only in Washington but in America's relationship around the world," and to "work in a partnership whenever we can, and alone only when he must." To prevent further deterioration in the relationship with Russia, Biden promised to "press the reset button" in an attempt to halt "a dangerous drift" in the relationship with America's old adversary.

During the early months of the new administration, Biden acted as a counselor on foreign policies and was responsible for gaining Senate support for Obama's legislative changes. His reputation for gaffes revived as his new position forced him to assume a public stance on a wide number of issues. Despite their starkly different personalities, Biden and Obama developed a close friendship.

The war in Afghanistan to root out al Qaeda terrorists was not going well, and the American generals were requesting more troops, beyond the twenty-one thousand Obama had already agreed to send. Top NATO and U.S. commander in Afghanistan, General Stanley McChrystal, warned that if more troops were not sent the next year, the defeat of the insurgents might not be possible. To respond to the growing threat of defeat, Obama and Biden held a series of intense meetings with military, diplomatic, and political advisors at Camp David. Biden acted as devil's advocate against the demands of the generals. Out of these meetings came a compromise giving McChrystal the additional troop surge, but with a deadline of July 2011 to start their withdrawal. Obama later commented on criticism of Biden's performance during the meetings and said, "I don't think anyone who was party to the very, very exhaustive discussions we had would say that. Joe was enormously helpful in guiding those discussions. The decision that ultimately emerged was a synthesis of some of the advice he gave me, along with the advice of the generals."

Chapter 6 – Second Term as Vice President

"For any young democracy, the most difficult but important step is burying the legacy of tyranny and establishing an economy and a government and institutions that abide by the rule of law. Every country faces challenges to the rule of law, including my own." - Joe Biden

In late 2011, the campaign had begun for a second term for President Obama and Vice President Biden. Early in the campaign there was some discussion of replacing Biden with Secretary of State Hillary Clinton, but White House officials later claimed Obama never seriously entertained the idea.

The controversial topic of same sex marriages became a campaign issue when Biden made an off-the-cuff remark that he was "absolutely comfortable" with same-sex marriages. Biden's comment upset Obama and his campaign officials, as this was a hot topic they were trying to avoid so as not to alienate the political right-leaning Christian voters. Gay rights advocates seized on Biden's remarks, and within days, Obama announced that he too supported same-sex marriage. Biden apologized to Obama in private for his impromptu public comments. The incident was just another time where Biden spoke from the heart rather than stuck with the script. Biden's lack of "message discipline" would prompt *Time* magazine to write, "Everyone knows [that] Biden's greatest strength is also his greatest weakness."

On January 20, 2013, Biden was inaugurated to a second term as vice president. During the first months in office, the administration tried to tackle the issues of gun violence, violence against women, and sexual harassment by developing stronger legislation. Biden worked on several other important legislative changes and managed to avoid controversy around his name.

During his second term, Biden continued to advocate for women. On January 22, 2014, the Vice President joined President Obama and created the White House Task Force to Protect Students from Sexual Assault. The Vice President co-chaired an interagency task force along with the White House Council on Women and Girls. Biden and the task force worked to partner across the government, education, academia, and communities to ensure that all students feel safe and can thrive when they are at school. Biden's advocacy for women goes back many years, to 1990, when he was a senator and introduced the Violence Against Women Act in Congress. The landmark legislation was passed into law in 1994, where it established new federal crimes of interstate domestic violence and stalking, doubled penalties for repeat sex offenders, and sparked the passage of laws at the state level to protect victims.

Figure – President Barack Obama presents Vice President Joe Biden with the Presidential Medal of Freedom with Distinction during a tribute to the vice president in the White House

President Obama surprised Vice President Biden on January 12, 2017, when he bestowed the Presidential Medal of Freedom on him, calling Mr. Biden "my brother" in a tearful ceremony in the East Room of the White House. The president had invited Biden and his wife to the White House for a private farewell; instead, the room was filled with his friends, family, and colleagues to witness the presentation of the nation's highest honor, the Presidential Medal of Freedom. Mr. Obama awarded the medal with an added level of veneration that previous presidents had reserved for recipients like Pope John Paul II and former Secretary of State Colin Powell. Mr. Obama said during the televised ceremony, "To know Joe Biden is to know love without pretense, service without self regard, and to live life fully." The citation with the medal noted the vice president's "charm, candor, unabashed optimism, and deep and abiding patriotism," as well as his "strength and grace to overcome great adversity." The citation called Biden one of the most "consequential vice presidents in American history." The clearly emotional Biden addressed Mr. Obama, standing beside him, saying he had never met anyone who had "the integrity and decency and the sense of other people's needs like you do."

Chapter 7 – Life After the Vice Presidency

"Our future cannot depend on the government alone. The ultimate solutions lie in the attitudes and the actions of the American people." - Joe Biden

Near the end of his second term as vice president, many suspected that Biden had the intention to run for the 2016 Democratic presidential nomination. However, as he was approaching the age of 72 in 2015 and his elder son, Beau, had recently died of brain cancer, Biden declared that he no longer had the energy to take on such a big commitment. On October 21, 2015, he officially announced his decision not to enter the race. When Obama endorsed Hillary Clinton, Biden decided to do the same. He also spoke very critically of the Republican candidate Donald Trump during the election and into Trump's term as president.

Figure - Delaware Attorney General Beau Biden at a Justice Department press conference in 2013

In February 2017, Joe and Jill Biden announced the formation of the Biden Foundation. In a video posted to the foundation's website, Joe Biden says the foundation will work to end violence against women on college campuses. In the video, he also states he will continue his "cancer moonshot," an effort kicked off by the Obama administration and approved by Congress in 2016. This effort continues Biden's fight against cancer, which he started after the loss of his son to brain cancer. "We are at an inflection point in the fight against cancer that didn't exist four or five years ago," said the former vice president. The foundation will focus its work in seven key areas: foreign policy; Biden's cancer initiative; community colleges and military families; protecting children; equality; ending violence against women; and strengthening the middle class. In a joint statement, Joe and Jill Biden said, "We look forward to this new chapter where we will continue our work to ensure that everyone—no matter their income level, race, gender, age, or sexuality—is treated with dignity and gets a fair shot at achieving the American Dream."

In November 2017, Joe Biden's new book, *Promise Me, Dad: A Year of Hope, Hardship, and Purpose,* was released. The book chronicles his personal and professional struggles the year after his son, Beau, was diagnosed with a malignant brain tumor. Beau had told his father, "Give me your word that no matter what happens, you're going to be all right." Joe Biden gave him his word. *The New York Times* writer, Jennifer Senior, wrote of Biden's book:

"What's most remarkable about Biden's Promise Me, Dad: A Year of Hope, Hardship, and Purpose *is that he's decided to give us full visibility into the agony and*

strangeness of that period, showing just what it was like to care for his son—and then mourn him—while simultaneously fulfilling his duties as vice president. The book is a backstage drama, honest, raw, and rich in detail. People who have lost someone will genuinely take comfort from what he has to say."

The End

Thank you for purchasing this book, and I hope you found it enjoyable. Please don't forget to leave a review for the book. I read every review and they help me become a better writer.

Doug West

Timeline

November 20, 1942 – Born Joseph Robinette Biden, Jr., in Scranton, Pennsylvania, to Joseph Robinette Biden, Sr. (a car salesman) and Catherine Eugenia (Finnegan) Biden. First of four siblings in a Catholic family.

1961- Graduates from Archmere Academy. Played football and elected class president two years.

1965 – Graduates from University of Delaware with a B.A. with a double major in history and political science.

August 27, 1966 – Marries Neilia Hunter.

1968 – Graduates from Syracuse University Law School with J.D.

1968-1970 - Defense attorney for criminal cases in Wilmington, Delaware.

1970-1972 - Serves on the New Castle County Council in Delaware.

1972 - Is first elected to the Senate at age 29, defeating Republican Senator J. Caleb Boggs. Wins re-election in 1978, 1984, 1990, 1996, 2002, and 2008.

December 18, 1972 - While Christmas shopping, Biden's first wife, Neilia Hunter Biden, and daughter Naomi Biden are killed in a car accident. His sons Beau and Hunter are badly injured, but survived.

January 5, 1973 - Sworn in as US senator of Delaware at son Beau's bedside in the hospital.

June 17, 1977 – Marries Jill Jacobs.

1987-1995 - Chairman of the Senate Committee on the Judiciary.

June 9, 1987 - Enters the 1988 presidential race, but drops out three months later following reports of plagiarism and false claims about his academic record.

February 1988 - Undergoes surgery to repair an aneurysm in an artery that supplies blood to the brain.

January 20, 1990 - Introduces a bill that becomes the Violence Against Women Act (VAWA). The act addresses sexual assault and domestic violence. It is signed into law by President Bill Clinton in 1994.

2001-2003 - Chairman of the Senate Foreign Relations Committee.

2002 - Votes to authorize military intervention in Iraq, but later becomes a vocal critic of the conflict.

2007-2009 - Chairman of the Senate Foreign Relations Committee.

January 31, 2007 - Files a statement of candidacy with the Federal Elections Commission to run for president.

August 1, 2007 - Releases his memoir, *Promises to Keep: On Life and Politics*.

January 3, 2008 - Announces his withdrawal from the presidential race.

August 23, 2008 - Is named the vice-presidential running mate of Barack Obama.

November 4, 2008 - Is elected vice president of the United States.

January 15, 2009 - Resigns from the Senate.

January 20, 2009 - Sworn in as vice president of the United States.

February 7, 2009 - Delivers first major speech as vice president at a security conference in Germany.

September 1, 2010 - Presides over a ceremony in Iraq to formally mark the end of the US combat mission in Iraq.

November 6, 2012 - President Obama and Biden are re-elected, defeating Republicans Mitt Romney and Paul Ryan.

January 20, 2013 - Is sworn in for his second term as vice president of the United States.

October 2, 2014 - Speaking at the John F. Kennedy School of Government at Harvard University, Biden tells attendees that ISIS has been inadvertently strengthened by actions taken by Turkey, the UAE, and other Middle Eastern allies to help opposition groups fighting against Syrian President Bashar al-Assad.

October 4, 2014 - Biden speaks by telephone with Turkish President Recep Tayyip Erdogan regarding remarks made at the John F. Kennedy School of Government. He apologizes "for any implication that Turkey or other allies and partners in the region had intentionally supplied or facilitated the growth of ISIL or other violent extremists in Syria."

May 30, 2015 - Biden's eldest son, Beau Biden, passes away from brain cancer at age 46.

October 21, 2015 - Announces he will not seek the presidency, stating that the window for a successful campaign "has closed."

January 12, 2017 - President Obama surprises Biden by presenting him with the Presidential Medal of Freedom, the nation's highest civilian honor, during a White House ceremony.

February 1, 2017 - Biden and his wife, Jill, launch the Biden Foundation, an organization that will work on seven issues: foreign policy; Biden's cancer initiative; community colleges and military families; protecting children; equality; ending violence against women; and strengthening the middle class.

February 7, 2017 - Is named the Benjamin Franklin presidential practice professor at the University of Pennsylvania, where he will lead the Penn Biden Center for Diplomacy and Global Engagement. He will also serve as the founding chair of the University of Delaware's Biden Institute.

March 1, 2017 - Biden receives the Congressional Patriot Award from the Bipartisan Policy Center. He receives the honor in recognition of his work crafting bipartisan legislation with Republicans and Democrats.

November 2017 – Releases bestselling book, *Promise Me, Dad: A Year of Hope, Hardship, and Purpose*.

References and Further Reading

Biden, Joe. *Promises to Keep: On Life and Politics*. Random House Trade Paperbacks. 2007.

Biden, Joe. *Promise Me, Dad: A Year of Hope, Hardship, and Purpose*. Flatiron Books. 2017.

Matuz, Roger. *The Presidents Fact Book: The Achievements, Campaigns, Events, Triumphs, Tragedies, and Legacies of Every President From George Washington to Barack Obama*. Black Dog & Leventhal Publishers, Inc. 2009.

Reeves, Thomas C. *Twentieth Century America: A Brief History*. Oxford University Press. 2000.

Senior, Jennifer. "Biden's Book: Private grief and its effect on public life." *The Kansas City Star*. November 26, 2017.

Witcover, Jules. *The American Vice Presidency: From Irrelevance to Power*. Smithsonian Books. 2014.

Internet References

Biden Withdraws Bid for President in Wake of Furor. *The New York Times*. Accessed November 9, 2017.

Campaign Portrait, Joe Biden: Orator for the Next Generation. *Time*. June 22, 1987. Accessed November 10, 2017.

It's official: Obama, Biden win second term. *Los Angeles Times*. January 4, 2013. Accessed November 10, 2017.

Joe Biden respected – if not always popular – for foreign policy record. *Los Angeles Times*. 24 August, 2008. Accessed November 10, 2017.

Senator Joseph Biden (Democrat, Delaware). U.S. State Department. Accessed November 10, 2017.

About Vice President Biden's Efforts to End Violence Against Women. The White House archives. Accessed December 30, 2017.

Merica, Dan. Joe, Jill Biden launch The Biden Foundation. CNN. February 1, 2017. Accessed December 30, 2017.

Vazquez, Maegan. Biden says he owes Anita Hill and apology. CNN. December 15, 2017. Accessed January 9, 2018.

Acknowledgments

I would like to thank Lisa Zahn for help in preparation of this book. All photographs are from the public domain. The quotes at the beginning of each chapter are from Brainyquote.com.

About the Author

Doug West is a retired aerospace engineer, small business owner, and experienced non-fiction writer with several books to his credit. His writing interests are general, with expertise in science, history, biographies, numismatics, and "How-to" topics. Doug has a B.S. in Physics from the Missouri School of Science and Technology and a Ph.D. in General Engineering from Oklahoma State University. He lives with his wife and little dog, "Scrappy," near Kansas City, Missouri. Additional books by Doug West can be found at http://www.amazon.com/Doug-West/e/B00961PJ8M. Follow the author on Facebook athttps://www.facebook.com/30minutebooks.

Figure – Doug West (photo by Karina West)

Additional Books by Doug West

Buying and Selling Silver Bullion Like a Pro
How to Write, Publish, and Market Your Own Audio Book
A Short Biography of the Scientist Sir Isaac Newton
A Short Biography of the Astronomer Edwin Hubble
Galileo Galilei – A Short Biography
Benjamin Franklin – A Short Biography
The Astronomer Cecilia Payne-Gaposchkin – A Short Biography
The American Revolutionary War – A Short History
Coinage of the United States – A Short History
John Adams – A Short Biography
In the Footsteps of Columbus (Annotated) Introduction and Biography Included (with Annie J. Cannon)
Alexander Hamilton – Illustrated and Annotated (with Charles A. Conant)
Harlow Shapley – Biography of an Astronomer
Alexander Hamilton – A Short Biography
The Great Depression – A Short History
Jesse Owens, Adolf Hitler and the 1936 Summer Olympics
Thomas Jefferson – A Short Biography
Gold of My Father – A Short Tale of Adventure
Making Your Money Grow with Dividend Paying Stocks – Revised Edition
The French and Indian War – A Short History
The Mathematician John Forbes Nash Jr. – A Short Biography
The British Prime Minister Margaret Thatcher – A Short Biography
Vice President Mike Pence – A Short Biography
President Jimmy Carter – A Short Biography
President Ronald Reagan – A Short Biography
President George H. W. Bush – A Short Biography

Dr. Robert H. Goddard – A Brief Biography - Father of American Rocketry and the Space Age
Richard Nixon: A Short Biography - 37th President of the United States
Charles Lindbergh: A Short Biography - Famed Aviator and Environmentalist
Dr. Wernher von Braun: A Short Biography - Pioneer of Rocketry and Space Exploration
Bill Clinton: A Short Biography – 42nd President of the United States

Index

www.ingramcontent.com/pod-product-compliance
Lightning Source LLC
LaVergne TN
LVHW010936030225
802818LV00002B/180

* 9 7 8 1 9 8 5 8 9 6 7 2 7 *